P9-CKJ-872

The LIGHT BOOK

The
LIGHT
BOOK

HOW NATURAL AND ARTIFICIAL LIGHT
AFFECT OUR HEALTH, MOOD, AND BEHAVIOR

JANE WEGSCHEIDER HYMAN

JEREMY P. TARCHER, INC.
Los Angeles

FH

. . . of making many books there is no end.

ECCLESIASTES

Library of Congress Cataloging in Publication Data

Hyman, Jane W.
  The light book / Jane W. Hyman.
    p. cm.
  ISBN 0-87477-559-0
  1. Radiation. 2. Light. 3. Electromagnetic waves.
QC475.H95 1990
535—dc20   89-49302
                                                          CIP
                                                          r89

Jeremy P. Tarcher, Inc.
5858 Wilshire Blvd., Suite 200
Los Angeles, CA 90036

Distributed by St. Martin's Press, New York

Design by Susan Shankin
Anatomical drawings by Edith Tagrin
All other illustrations by Kevin King

Manufactured in the United States of America
10 9 8 7 6 5 4 3 2 1

First Edition

CONTENTS

ACKNOWLEDGMENTS

This book was a group effort. From the idea of writing a book on this theme (Richard J. Wurtman) to overseeing and editing the manuscript (Connie Zweig), I am indebted to others. Helen Rees and Catherine Mahar guided me through the process of publishers and contracts. Becky Conekin at the Countway Library of Medicine, as well as Hans W. Wendt and Beverly Hurney, searched for and sent studies. Mary Waggener, Andee Rubin, Jack Hyman, Charles Hyman, Deborah Johnson, Heidi Blocher, Marie Cantlon, Peggy Schoditsch, and the women of the Boston Women's Health Book Collective provided encouragement, enthusiasm, and good advice.

The researchers listed below critiqued the manuscript, adding their invaluable expertise to the text. Included below are also those who had personal experiences with one of the topics discussed and who gave their time to be interviewed so that I could quote their experiences and learn from them. Many others whose names are not included sent studies and provided information by telephone.

My thanks to you all.

Janis Anderson
David Beyer
Connie Breece
Salvatore Capobianco
Ronald A. Chez
Richard G. Condon
Germaine Cornélissen
Vincent DeLeo
Leland N. Edmunds, Jr.
Christopher Fanta
Mark Fisher
Laurie Friedman
William Gange

Effie Graham
Linda Griffin
Franz Halberg
Ruth Harwood
Erhard Haus
J. Allan Hobson
Michael F. Holick
William J. M. Hrushesky
James I. Hudson
Carol Hutchinson
Daniel F. Kripke
Margaret L. Kripke
Sarah Leibowitz

Alfred J. Lewy
Ethel Lipnak
Diane McCarrick
Douglas G. McMahon
Joseph Majzoub
Timothy H. Monk
Till Roenneberg
Esther Rome
Lawrence E. Scheving
Diana Siegal
Sons of Norway, Norumbega
    Lodge Chapter, Massachusetts
Matilda Spitzer

Ruthann P. Sturtevant
Swedish Women's Educational
    Association (SWEA), Boston
    Chapter
Norma Swenson
Barbara Tate-Ostroff
Michael Terman
Nancy Thurson
Ann Voda
David Welsh
Rütger A. Wever
Seymour Zigman
Mary Zoll

FOREWORD

AS THE NEW century approaches, we are at the threshold of a major biomedical achievement—a practical handle on the physiology of time—that is going to modify the way we structure our living habits and environment. Ancient folklore notwithstanding, it has taken a generation of arduous animal and human laboratory experimentation to clarify the underlying principles of the brain's internal timekeeping system and its specific sensitivity to light input from the external world.

This knowledge arrives not one moment too soon: urbanized lifestyles and the confinement of indoor work activities have created a host of problems due to the simple factor of daylight deprivation. Now we see that our biological clock is vulnerable, and that it responds by triggering symptoms as diverse as sleep disturbances, waves of fatigue and lapses of alertness, appetite swings and difficulties maintaining weight, depressed mood, and more.

Nature, too, precipitates a daylight-deprivation syndrome in the temperate latitudes where most of us live. The body's biological clock is sensitive to the seasonal variations in length of night and day, sometimes with the serious consequences of winter depression. New clinical studies show that from 5 to 10 percent of the population in the mid- to northern United States becomes seriously disabled between December and February, when nights are longest. The symptoms include sluggishness, difficulty awakening, carbohydrate craving, and psychological responses of sadness, social withdrawal, low sexual desire, and work disturbance. The concern goes far beyond the so-called clinical population: many more people experience these seasonal swings as milder yet still bothersome "winter doldrums," which are far less common further south where outdoor light-dark cycles are more constant throughout the year.

The remarkable practical achievement of the last decade has been the development of artificial bright-light treatment, which can quickly trick the brain into operating in its summer mode, alleviating symptoms within a few days. That this can occur without drugs or psychotherapy—and after such short treatment—underscores our intimate physiological reliance on the external lighting environment. The technique presages, I believe, revolutions in both indoor lighting design and mental-health technology.

In this book, Jane W. Hyman charts the course of these and related discoveries in a unique integration of cutting-edge research in photobiology and its intersections with chronobiology, psychiatry, internal medicine, gynecology, pediatrics, geriatrics, cardiology, oncology, dermatology, and ophthalmology. She has gone directly to the scientists and defines their common ground and research thrust. She artfully reveals the historical trends, predating biomedical science, that have led us to this pregnant moment. And, with great sensitivity, she allows the sufferers of daylight deprivation to describe their own experiences and solutions. This is a book that is likely to change your behavior.

Michael Terman, Ph.D.
New York State Psychiatric Institute
Columbia University
March 1990

*I shed years in the summer, and feel a lot older in the
winter. The sun always has been relaxing and
energizing for me and I really miss it in the winter.
Just sitting in the sun for a few minutes has an
immediate effect on me. It's almost uncanny.*

59-YEAR-OLD MAN

*On bright moonlit nights I have a restless kind of
sleep. I have a large picture window in my bedroom,
and I don't see the moon, but I see the bright
moonlight. I think it's the bright light as much as
anything that wakens me.*

80-YEAR-OLD WOMAN

OUR LIVES ARE dominated by the relationship of the
earth to the sun and moon, our natural sources of light.
We associate the cycles of day and night, the tides, the months,
and the seasons of the year with the earth's and the moon's
rotations and revolutions. Countless aspects of our mental and
physical health are influenced by the rhythms of light that strike
the earth. The earth rotates on its axis every 24 hours, so that
each dawn brings sunlight, subtly varying in angle and intensity
throughout the day. The earth revolves around the sun every
365.25 days, determining our yearly patterns of light and darkness. Seasonal changes in light occur because of the earth's tilted
axis (see Figure 1).

Simultaneously, the moon goes through its phases, pro-
viding varying degrees of illumination at night. The moon revolves around the earth in about 29.5 days. Half of the moon is
always lit by the sun, but as the moon orbits the earth, different
amounts of its lighted part are visible to us. The darkness of the

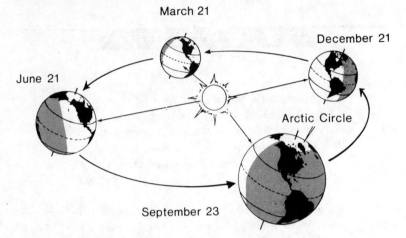

Figure 1. *The earth's orbit. From March to September the North Pole is tilted toward the sun, giving the Northern Hemisphere more sunlight than the Southern Hemisphere. From September to March the North Pole is tilted away from the sun, giving the Southern Hemisphere more sunlight. The closer we live to the North or South Pole, the more extreme are the relations between the hours of light and darkness. In the polar regions, either daylight or darkness is constant around the time of the two solstices. In regions above and below the equator, the hours of light and darkness are equal only at the spring and fall equinoxes. At the equator there is no seasonal change in daylight, always 12 hours of light and 12 of darkness.*

new-moon phase is followed by a crescent of visible light that gradually expands (waxes), becoming the quarter and full moons. After the moon has reached its maximum in light, it gradually darkens (wanes).

In recognizing the importance of light in our lives we lag behind our ancestors. Although the following chapters discuss new research on light and health, people's beliefs in the powers of the sun's and moon's light are among the oldest observations of recorded human history. In the past, natural light was honored through religions. Amon, Apollo, Artemis, Aurora, Diana, Eos, Freya, Helios, Horus, Hyperion, Luna, Re, Selena, Shamash, Sol, and Thoth are only a few of the names under which the personified sun, moon, and dawn have been worshipped. Some

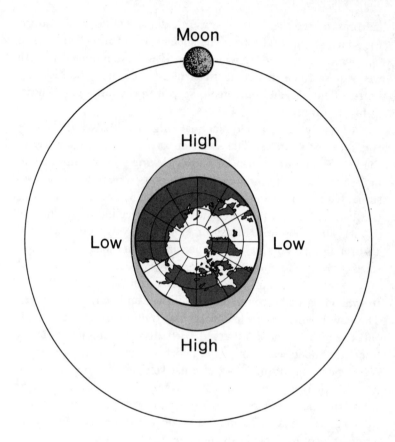

Figure 2. *The tides. As the earth rotates on its axis, different areas of its surface face the moon every 24 hours. Because the moon's gravity pulls at water and at the earth's center, it causes two high tides simultaneously: one on the side of the earth nearest the moon, and one on the side opposite the moon. The former is caused by the moon's pull on water, while the latter is caused by the moon's pull on the earth's center, creating a bulge between earth and water. Water flows from the other sides of the earth toward the moon's pull, causing corresponding low tides.*

High tides vary in their force. The most powerful, called spring tides, occur at the full and new moons; the weaker, called neap tides, occur at the first- and last-quarter moons. These variations are caused by the periodic alignment of the sun, moon, and earth, so that the sun's gravity pulls in the same direction as the moon's gravity during the full and new moons.

cultures revered the sun-god as the creator and father of all things, the source of all vital force. The ancient Mexicans called the sun Spalnemohuani, "He by whom men live."[1] They fueled it with frequent sacrifice, believing that the sun required the bleeding hearts of animals and humans to keep it in the full vigor of heat, light, and motion.[2]

Many peoples held biannual religious rituals at the winter and summer solstices. The summer solstice, the longest day of the year, is the sun's turning point. Having climbed higher and higher for half the year, the sun begins its way downward. Presumably, ancient peoples observed this phenomenon with fear and believed they could prevent the sun's decline by rekindling it with large bonfires. Midsummer fire festivals were once held all over Europe and are still important celebrations in some European towns and throughout Norway.

For a period of about 3000 years, from around 5000 B.C., the moon as deity commanded political and religious power.[3] The new moon was greeted with joy, the full moon celebrated, and the waning moon observed with anxiety. Among its many roles, the moon was seen as the beneficent guardian of the menstrual cycle and of birth; or, alternatively, as the cruel god who monthly defiled women. In connection with the dew, rain, and tides, the moon was believed to promote growth in plants, animals, and humans. The moon's influence on life continues to be a persistently held belief in many parts of the world.[4]

Religious honors to the sun and moon were reflected in ancient knowledge of the body. In the Western world, rhythms in body functions that imitate the cycles of the earth and moon have been suspected since at least 400 B.C., when Hippocrates recorded his observations on daily and seasonal rhythms in physical and mental health. In eastern Asia, Chinese health-care practitioners have long recognized that the body changes during the course of each day, with the seasons of the year, and, in women, with the stages of the menstrual cycle. For over 5000 years traditional Chinese medicine has taken such rhythms into account.[5] These beliefs and practices based on the relevance of light to life

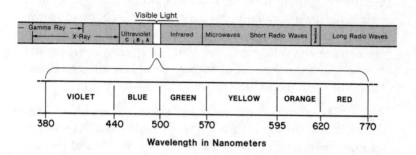

Figure 3. *The spectrum of electromagnetic radiation. "Light" refers to waves of electromagnetic energy called radiation. Radiation is made up of photons, particles that cause change when they collide with atoms or molecules such as those in our bodies. The sun transmits its energy through space in the form of radiation that produces change in living things including plants, insects, animals, and humans. Sunlight is composed of all the colors of the rainbow. Each color corresponds to a wavelength of light measured in nanometers. (One nanometer is a billionth of a meter.) "Visible light" refers to the wavelengths that the human eye can see.*

and health predate by centuries the scientific evidence of their truth.

Current research clarifies the ways in which the sun and moon influence our health. Light coordinates the body chemicals that govern the way we sleep, feel, and behave. As each day proceeds and the level of daylight changes, these chemicals fluctuate, altering our alertness and capacity for physical and mental tasks. As daylight becomes shorter or longer with the changing seasons, some body chemicals also shift their timing. These shifts often cause seasonal changes in mood, energy, sleep, and susceptibility to certain illnesses and diseases. In some people, these changes can be so powerful that they become health problems requiring medical care.

Light may influence our reproductive health by affecting the timing of puberty, the menstrual cycle, and rhythms in fertility and childbirth. Fluctuations in weight can be seasonal,

5

and certain kinds of food craving and binge-eating are related to the effects of light on the rhythms of appetite-controlling chemicals in the brain. Sunlight can strengthen our bones by triggering the body's process of vitamin D production. Simultaneously, light can damage the skin, eyes, and immune system, a danger that increases with the destruction in the stratosphere of ozone, which filters the sun's harmful rays.

The effects of the sun and moon on our health add new dimensions to our comprehension of our own bodies. As researchers examine the significance of light in our mental and physical health, they uncover the wisdom behind early beliefs and observations. The following pages chart this rediscovery. Besides honoring our ancestors' wisdom, this book serves as a guide toward better health through understanding the effects of light on the functioning of our bodies.

CHAPTER 1

Sunlight: The Giver of Time

ACCORDING TO GREEK myth, the nymph Clytie wasted away of unrequited love for the sun-god Helios. She never stirred from the bare ground, never tasted food or drink, but only gazed on Helios, turning her face to follow him as he rode his chariot across the sky. Her limbs, they say, became rooted to the earth, and a lavender flower grew over her face.[1] To this day the flower opens to Helios at sunrise, turns on its stem to face him on his travels, and closes when the god departs at dusk. The flower came to be called a heliotrope, in honor of the god of the sun.

In ancient Greece, this myth explained the secret of why some plants appear to praise the sun with their daily movements. The Greeks believed that the heliotrope responds directly to the sun, and that it would remain closed in the absence of sunlight. This assumption was not challenged until 1729, when a French scientist placed a heliotrope plant in a dark closet and observed that it continued its daily motions in time with the sun's passage across the sky. The scientist urged his colleagues to pursue the study of this new mystery: a plant that "responds to the sun without being exposed to it any way."[2]

Researchers did not follow this advice until the twentieth century, when they began uncovering 24-hour and other rhythmic cycles in plants, insects, animals, and within the human body. Scientists are now proving that we participate in the time structure of the planets, with the relative motions of the earth, moon, and sun reflected in the rhythms of our bodies.

THE DAY WITHIN

As the heliotrope illustrates, the primary rhythm is the 24-hour rotation of the earth, bringing sunrise and sunset. So essential to life is this planetary rhythm that a system for keeping time with it is built into our bodies. This is called the *circadian system,* from the Latin *circa* meaning approximately, and *dies* meaning day. This system is like a network of internal clocks that times and coordinates events within our bodies according to an approximate 24-hour cycle. This cycle corresponds to the time it takes the earth to spin on its axis, exposing all of life to daily rhythms of light, darkness, and temperature. All of us have circadian timing systems, each one keeping its own approximate 24-hour schedule, or "day within."[3]

Our bodies may begin measuring time before birth. In animals, and perhaps in humans, the fetus is first cued to the 24-hour cycle in the womb.[4] Nutrients and hormones regularly cross the placenta and enter the bloodstream of the fetus. This flow from the mother, as well as her body temperature and activities, reflect her circadian rhythms, and the fetus cues its internal day according to hers. After birth, the newborn continues to learn essential rhythms from the mother, perhaps through nursing, until its own circadian system is fully developed and cued to the light-dark cycle.

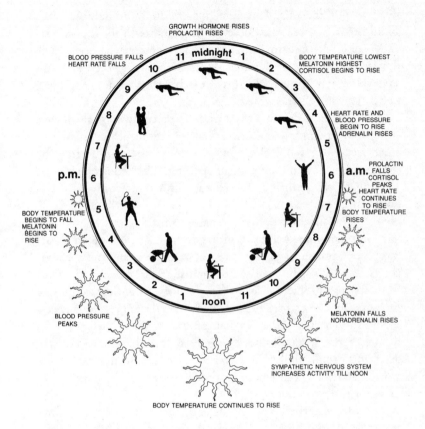

Figure 4. *The day within: A sample of the body's daily rhythms.*

The 24-hour cycle of light and darkness played such a fundamental role in the development of life that a built-in sense of time is present in virtually all plants and animals, from algae to humans. Even some single-celled organisms have 24-hour or near-24-hour timekeeping systems. Researchers think that circadian rhythms are as old as life itself, enabling selected organisms to function in time to astronomical rhythms. A sense of time is crucial to survival on a rhythmic planet, and in the course of evolution presumably only those organisms with circadian rhythms

9

lived to tell the tale. Circadian systems tell the deer when to avoid predators, tell the goose when to fly south for the winter, and enable the bee to learn when each flower will open. The precise scheduling of these events is necessary to each animal's survival. If it is the early bird that catches the worm, a bird must know how to tell the time of day.

Plants are equally rhythmic. So precisely do some flowers time their opening and closing that an eighteenth-century botanist created a living clock by planting flowers in a circle by species according to their time of opening. The heliotrope is itself a living clock, pointing toward the sun's position even in 24-hour darkness.

The circadian system prepares us for the start of each new day. For example, before it grows light and we awaken, heart rate, blood pressure, and body temperature rise, and the hormone cortisol, which helps us defend against stress, starts to increase from its low nighttime level. This ability to anticipate and be prepared for the transition from dark to light enabled our ancestors to survive the challenges that came with dawn, such as battle, flight, or the strenuous search for food. Similar challenges still exist for people living in poverty or in war-torn areas of the world, and for those whose workday begins in the darkness or dawn of early morning.

Because the body's fluids and tissues function according to circadian rhythms, our physical and mental abilities differ widely from one time of day to another. Competence in tasks at school or at work fluctuates, since the rhythms of body chemicals influence mood, alertness, and manual dexterity. For example, the ability to do tasks requiring verbal reasoning and short-term memory, such as arguing a case or taking an exam, tends to peak toward late morning or midday. However, we are better off studying for the exam between six and twelve in the evening, when our long-term memorization is strongest.[5] Repetitive tasks involving manual dexterity, such as some forms of assembly-line work or practicing scales on the piano, tend to be easiest during the late afternoon and evening.[6] In general, we tend to be better

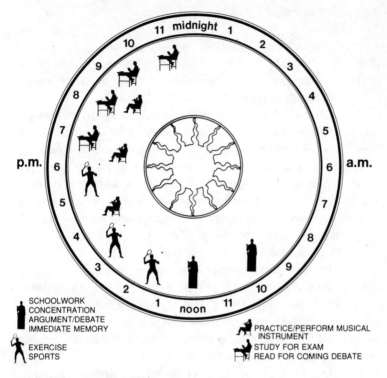

Figure 5. *Daily peaks in performance.*

at strictly mental work (except for memorization) in the forenoon, while the body prefers physical tasks in the later part of the day. In all cases, however, the body's peak reaction times can vary individually in those who have a strong tendency to be a "morning" person or an "evening" person. (See "Light-Related Sleep Problems" in chapter 3.)

The Structure of the Circadian System

If you lived in a cave, away from sunlight and all other clues as to the time of day, your "day within" would become 25 hours long. This 25-hour inner day is the basis for the term "circadian": an approximate day. This approximate rather than exact timing probably serves to make the system more easily

11

adjustable to fluctuating time cues such as the sun's seasonal changes in rising and setting. Researchers call this 25-hour cycle a "free-running" condition: the body's innate rhythm independent of sunlight or other time cues from the environment.

After a few weeks in the cave, your body's rhythms might also split apart from one another, or desynchronize. While some hormones and other body chemicals would continue their 25-hour cycles, your sleep-wake cycle might break away. Your cycle of activity and rest, normally 24 hours, could shorten to 16 or lengthen to 30. For example, one woman who spent four months in a cave for an experiment tended to be awake and active 20 to 25 hours at a stretch, then sleep 10 hours, making her daily cycle 30 to 35 hours long.[7]

In order to run precisely according to the 24-hour day, the circadian system must have a time cue from the environment. That cue is usually sunlight, which daily "sets the clock" and synchronizes the body's complex web of rhythms to correspond to the 24-hour cycle of light and darkness. Sunlight is a *zeitgeber*, or giver of time.

Light enters the retina of the eye, which acts as an extension or antenna of the brain. From the retina, electrical impulses in nerve cells transmit signals of light and dark through special pathways to the hypothalamus and to other regions of the brain. Research suggests that one of the most important internal timekeepers is located in the hypothalamus. It consists of two clusters of nerve cells called the suprachiasmatic nuclei, or SCN. A direct tract leads from the retina to these two clusters of cells. The SCN have cells that respond to the light signals from the retina. These cells or others in the SCN send electrical and chemical messages to other parts of the brain and body, reporting the time of day (see Figure 6).

The SCN is called an oscillator or pacemaker because it sets the pace of the body's various rhythms, keeping them coordinated with one another and with the earth's rotation. Many researchers think that we have at least one other pacemaker in the brain, perhaps within the SCN itself. The SCN evidently sends information through electrical/chemical impulses to a number of other tissues, including other areas of the hypothalamus, the pituitary, pineal, and parts of the brain stem. These tissues in turn send hormonal messages to other control systems in the body—for example, the heart, adrenal glands, liver, kidney, and intestines—keeping them in time with the pacemaker(s).

The *zeitgeber*, or time cue, that synchronizes the entire system of rhythms is usually the sun. Other time cues, such as acoustical signals (e.g., an alarm clock) and a regular schedule of sleeping, waking, and eating may help reinforce the *zeitgeber*. The pacemaker can be reset by the use of unusually bright artificial light. The timing of the light is critical. Light during the dawn hours resets the pacemaker to an earlier hour, while light in the evening resets it to a later hour. Light in the middle of the day has little or no effect on the pacemaker.

The Three Eyes

> The soul has its principal seat in the small gland
> [pineal] located in the middle of the brain. From
> there it radiates through the rest of the body by
> means of the animal spirits, the nerves, and even
> the blood. . . . The slightest movements on the
> part of this gland may alter very greatly the course
> of these spirits.
>
> DESCARTES, 1649[8]

The retina evolved as a protrusion of the brain. It functions, in part, as the starting point of the body's circadian system and appears to respond most sensitively to the green portion of the light spectrum. The retina's light-receiving cells apparently change their structure during the day and may regulate the light information they receive. Therefore, the circadian rhythms of retinal cells possibly determine the time of day our eyes are most sensitive to light.

Two of the eye's most light-sensitive times appear to be

the twilight of dawn and dusk. The length of the twilight hours varies with the seasons. Findings suggest that the eye is exquisitely sensitive to the length of twilight and registers the current and approaching seasons accordingly.[9] In this way the retina may obtain beginning-of-day, beginning-of-night, and season-of-year information during the twilight period. These are vital pieces of information for the body's daily and seasonal rhythms of chemicals.

Since the eyes play a key role as the brain's windows to the world, those who are blind due to damage to the retina can have dramatically unstable circadian rhythms, experiencing uncontrollable waves of fatigue at a later time each day. On the other hand, some of the sightless remain in rhythm with the 24-hour day. The retino-hypothalamic tract through which light transmits its time signals to the brain is separate from the visual pathway. It is therefore possible to be functionally blind yet timed according to the light-dark cycle. Conversely, some people with excellent vision are unable to adjust to the 24-hour light-dark cycle, perhaps due to dysfunction of the retino-hypothalamic tract.

One of the most interesting hormones in the study of biological rhythms is called melatonin. It is secreted by the pineal gland, a small cone-shaped structure behind the midbrain (see Figure 6). The pineal has long fascinated researchers. It has been thought to have unique, somewhat mysterious functions. Descartes, the French philosopher and scientist quoted above, believed that the pineal could see light and that essential exchanges between the outer and inner worlds took place in this gland.[10]

Current research suggests that the essence of Descartes's theory is correct. The pineal gland secretes melatonin rhythmically, in time with the 24-hour light-dark cycle. Melatonin reaches its highest levels in darkness and reacts directly to sunlight, which suppresses its flow. Recent findings indicate that melatonin influences biological rhythms by acting directly on a pacemaker or biological clock within the SCN of the hypothalamus.[11] In this way melatonin may modulate the body's rhythmic coordination

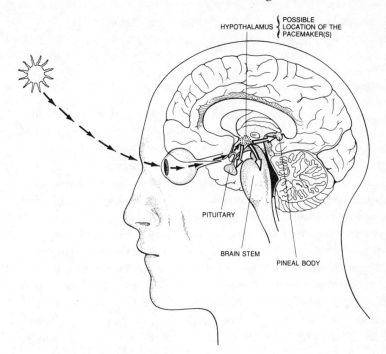

Figure 6. *From the sun to the brain.*

to the 24-hour light-dark cycle and the seasons. Some researchers suspect that melatonin has the specific purpose of registering darkness in the environment.

Possibly the pineal gland evolved from the parietal eye of certain reptiles, a part of the animal's pineal that extends upward from the organ like a miniature telescope and slightly protrudes from the center of the head. This "third eye" is not a seeing eye, yet it has a lens and retina and provides information about light to the animal's brain. In some vertebrates, the pineal gland and parietal eye are part of the body's timekeeping system and influence the animal's exposure to sunlight, body temperature, aggressiveness, and courting/mating rituals. Most researchers believe that the pineal's influence is exerted through its production of melatonin, modified by the parietal eye. This function of the "third eye" is integrated into our seeing eyes.

Other Biological Rhythms

The circadian system is one of many biological rhythms in the body. The circadian rhythm is reflected in the sleep-wake cycle, in the rise and fall of body temperature and blood pressure, and in the daily fluctuations of numerous hormones.

The body has many other rhythms, both shorter and longer than 24 hours. Brain waves and the tempo of heartbeats oscillate in periods of less than a day, called *ultradian* rhythms. Women menstruate in periods averaging 29.5 days, and new skin cells rise to the surface of the skin every 29 days. Such rhythms of approximately one month are called *circalunar*. Menstrual rhythms may be influenced by the lunar as well as the solar cycle (see chapter 2, "Fertility and Childbirth"). The body also has seasonal or *circannual* rhythms. For example, studies suggest that the heart responds with more ease to the challenge of exercise in the spring and summer compared to winter. [12] Evidently our lungs are also at their best in summer, capable of taking in more oxygen than in winter. Many of the body's chemicals, such as cortisol, testosterone, thyroxine, and serotonin, have yearly fluctuations. The adjustments of these and other chemicals to seasonal changes in light affect our health, mood, sleep, and sexuality, as discussed in subsequent chapters.

The daily, monthly, and yearly rhythms reflect the cycles of the earth, sun, and moon. However, the body's immune system also has a rhythm of an approximate week, called a *circaseptan* rhythm (see chapter 7, "Wellness and Disease"). This intriguing rhythm does not imitate any pattern found in the planets' rotations. Instead, it may have evolved as a special time structure to integrate other rhythms within the body. However, researchers debate whether the circaseptan rhythm is built into the body or imposed on the body through our calendar.

Some evidence suggests that all biological rhythms are locked together by the daily signal of sunlight or other time cues to the same pacemaker, although this is a controversial theory. Daily, seasonal, and other rhythms may require multiple pacemakers, regulated by light and other time cues in different ways.

Biological rhythms are evidently built into our bodies as part of the genetic code, just like the color of our eyes or the ability to learn to speak. Researchers have discovered a "rhythm gene" in the strand of DNA (deoxyribonucleic acid) in animals. DNA contains the body's genetic code.

THE IMPACT OF URBAN LIFE

Some researchers think that a smoothly running circadian system, well synchronized to the light-dark cycle, is the foundation of health. The following chapters illustrate the basis of this belief. Yet our lives are full of influences on circadian rhythms, many of them inherent in technology and city life. We evolved as a species over several million years in a light-dark cycle regulated solely by astronomical rhythms. Therefore, whenever we switch on bright electric lights in the middle of the night we confound our bodies' evolutionary experience. Studies show that the normal lamplight we use routinely in our homes and workplaces can influence the circadian rhythms of the body's chemicals[13] and even synchronize them.[14] Researchers are still debating the implications of these findings, since it was previously thought that only artificial light of unusual brightness and intensity could synchronize the circadian system. Possibly each person's unique sensitivity to light causes some to synchronize by ordinary room light and others not. Unusually bright artificial light of about 2500 lux (see Glossary) or greater is indisputably a powerful synchronizer.

Other aspects of our daily lives or our surroundings can also influence circadian rhythms. They include the following:

17

Electromagnetic fields. The circadian system is sensitive to electromagnetic fields, waves of electrically charged particles such as radio waves, infrared and ultraviolet light, X rays, and gamma rays. The earth's atmosphere generates electromagnetic fields, and the visible light of the sun is itself such a field. In the absence of sunlight, other sources of electromagnetic fields can alter the timing of rhythms and, if periodically switched on and off, possibly synchronize them. The human body also generates electromagnetic fields, and some researchers suspect that circadian rhythms respond to these as well, although this is a controversial point.

Data suggest that those who live or work near power lines with extremely low-frequency electric and magnetic fields may have an increased risk of desynchronized rhythms, causing symptoms similar to jet lag, or even depression.[15] However, there is still no proof that electromagnetic fields are the cause of these problems.

Stress. Psychological burdens appear to influence circadian rhythms, altering the timing and increasing the tendency toward internal desynchronization.

Chemicals. Animal studies suggest that certain chemicals in food and drugs have the power to alter the circadian system. This research indicates that body temperature rhythms can be set backward or forward like a clock, depending on the drug used and the time in the circadian cycle when it is administered.[16] Ethanol, the alcoholic constituent of wine, beer, and liquor, is one such drug. It is possible that methylxanthines, found in coffee, tea, chocolate, and some soft drinks and over-the-counter drugs, can also alter rhythms, but this research is disputed.

Insecticides and other environmental pollutants may also alter biological rhythms, a finding of special concern because of our chronic exposure to such poisons.

Medications and medical technology. Some frequently prescribed drugs may affect circadian rhythms. Such drugs include Halcion and perhaps other anti-anxiety and sleep-inducing drugs (benzodiazepines); reserpine, given for high blood pressure and anxiety; certain beta-blockers, usually given for high blood pressure; and lithium, given for some forms of mood disorders. The extent of each drug's effects on rhythms may depend on the time of day it is taken. (See chapter 7, "Wellness and Disease.")

Therapies such as radiation for breast cancer can alter some circadian rhythms, leaving others stable. X rays may have a similar influence.

Added to these appendages of modern life are central heating, windowless offices, 24-hour convenience stores, air travel, and shift work, all of which can confuse the body's rhythms so intricately attuned to sunrise and sunset. Technology has changed the world for which our bodies were designed. Such changes come at a price to our health.

Studies show that when we ignore the 24-hour light-dark cycle and keep irregular hours of work and rest, rhythms go awry and alertness declines. [17] This is true even if a person gets a total of eight hours sleep every 24 hours. Some research suggests that long-term attempts to live according to time periods widely different from 24 hours can shorten the life span. [18]

Even the minor deviations in timing of weekday and weekend life can confuse the circadian system, perhaps accounting for the Monday morning "hangover" many of us experience as our bodies try to readjust. Some of us work in windowless offices, isolating ourselves from the time cues of sunlight. Many of us travel by air for business and pleasure. When such travel takes us across time zones, the actual day-night cycle suddenly shifts, while our internal rhythms remain on the old time. How long it takes our bodies to adjust depends on the direction of travel (east to west is easier on the system than west to east), our age, and the strength or stubbornness of the circadian system. Some people take up to 18 days to readjust to a trip across six time zones—in other words, three days per hour of time change. [19] To make matters worse, when we fly on business rather than pleasure we are often expected to be alert, persuasive, and to make important decisions shortly after arrival. On a business trip from New York to Paris, this can mean trying to be at our best when our body time is 4:00 A.M.

The following suggestions can help minimize the effects of jet lag.[20]

- Be well rested prior to your flight.
- Consider gradually changing your bedtime and arising by one hour or less per day toward the new routine. (Do this only if it is possible without losing sleep.)
- On boarding the plane, immediately set your watch to the new time zone and try to adjust your activity according to that time; for example, sleep when it is nighttime at your destination.
- On arrival, get out and about in the daylight.
- Try to stay up until the bedtime of your destination. If sleep is irresistible before then, take an afternoon nap but set your alarm for a maximum of two hours.
- For trips of only a day or two, consider staying on your home routine if you can schedule meetings and events accordingly. In this case, you do the opposite of the suggestions listed above: keep your watch on the old time; remain indoors as much as possible; and stay strictly on your home routine.

Some researchers are beginning to study the possibility of light therapy to reduce jet lag. Conceivably, artificial light could help recycle the circadian system before departure so that the traveler arrives at the destination already synchronized to the local time. Taking the hormone melatonin at carefully planned times is also under study as a method of alleviating jet lag.

Remaining close to home does not protect us from sudden time shifts. Twice a year the entire population of more than 25 countries is subjected to the shift of daylight savings time systems. The shift of only one hour may seem trivial, yet it takes several days for internal rhythms to adjust completely. Many of us notice how sleep, alertness, and mood can be affected by the

> knotted thirty times,—so
>   the bound twig that's under-
>   gone and over-gone, can't stir.
>
> The weak overcomes its
>   menace, the strong over-
>   comes itself. What is there
>
> like fortitude! What sap
>   went through that little thread
>   to make the cherry red!

The import of this poem is only gradually realized, and then not by way of similitude or metaphor, but directly, as a statement forced into full consciousness by the poet's sheer sense of the facts of the life in these natural objects. Even so, she cannot end with her simply humane sense of what all this means to her. She begins with objects, turns inward to the self, and then returns to objects. It is the cherry red to which she returns, as she has begun with the strawberry. The method is that of analogy, we can say; but we must note how the analogy exists for the sake of the scene and not vice-versa, as we would expect in the meditative-descriptive mode. Moreover, there is no transformation worked on the materials of the scene; the poet does not take possession of them, so to read herself in terms of them. We cannot but remark the poet's polite and lady-like presence: again in the delightfully "arbitrary" quality of the form and metrics and in the absolute control they manifest. The effect is, however, of the poet who is fully in control of herself and is unwilling to control anyone or anything else. She tries neither to convince nor celebrate. She tries only to know—to know her world, and in the act to know herself (and presumably others like her). The poem defines nothing but what it is to make this particular poem on this particular occasion in this particular scene. We may well recall:

> The wave may go over it if
> it likes.
> Know that it will be there when it says,
>   "I shall be there when the wave has gone by."

There is, finally, a curious lack of commitment here. When we think of Williams, Aiken, Cummings, and (as we shall presently) Stevens, we may well regret the lack. But we may well be grateful for other things: above all, for the fact that she, more than any other American poet of her time respects (in a phrase dear to Stevens) "things as they are." She is most certainly not tormented, as are the other poets with whom I have grouped her, by things as they are. She will neither appropriate nor be appropriated by them. The world in whose ineluctably objective existence she would find her own, as she wrote in an early poem "New York," is not one of "plunder, / but 'accessibility to experience.' " The phrase, she acknowledged in one of her puzzlingly honest notes, is Henry James'. Realizing this, one puts her on the side of the Newmans and even the Strethers of this world. Why all the fuss? she seems, in her quite feminine realism, to be saying. She concludes another early poem "England" thus:

> The sublimated wis-
>   dom
> of China, Egyptian discernment, the catalysmic torrent of
>   emotion compressed
> in the verbs of the Hebrew language, the books of the man
>   who is able
>
> to say, "I envy nobody but him, and him only, who catches
>   more fish than
> I do,"—the flower and fruit of all that noted superi-
> ority—should one not have stumbled upon it in America,
>   must one imagine
> that it is not there? It has never been confined to one local-
>   ity.

A place, a time, and a condition occasion humanity. Attending to the intrinsic requirements of place, time, and condition, one attends to—one stumbles upon—his humanity. Beyond this, Miss Moore seems not to want to go. She knows only (or, will let herself know only) what it is to say yes! yes! yes! (Her yes! is muted, cautious, and somewhat finicking, to be sure, but it is as authentic as Molly Bloom's.) It has never occurred to her, one imagines, to say no! no! no!—not even to say no! so that she can all the more fully and freely say yes!

Meditation and Enactment

by Hugh Kenner

Miss Moore's formalisms are so tactful they will not make themselves heard. Not everything, she seems to say, must emerge as talk, talk. And so this is, more or less, what we hear:

> There is a great amount of poetry in unconscious fastidiousness.
> Certain Ming products,
> imperial floor-coverings of coach-wheel yellow,
> are well enough in their way
> but I have seen something that I like better—
> a mere childish attempt to make an imperfectly ballasted animal
>   stand up,
> similar determination to make a pup eat his meal from the plate.

While this, on the other hand, is what we see:

> There is a great amount of poetry in unconscious
>   fastidiousness. Certain Ming
>   products, imperial floor-coverings of coach-
>   wheel yellow, are well enough in their way but I have seen
>   something
>   that I like better—a
>   mere childish determination to make an imperfectly ballasted
>   animal stand up,
>
>   similar determination to make a pup
>   eat his meal from the plate.

"Up," this encourages us to notice, rhymes with "pup"; and if we wonder whether "Ming" was meant to rhyme with "something," we have only to check lines 2 and 4 of the remaining stanzas of "Critics and Connoisseurs" to make sure that it was. Awareness of these details may affect our vocalization, but not much; the eye of curiosity discovers them, the mind of affection retains them, but for the voice to force them on another person's notice entails such a disruption of sense as to constitute a breach of manners. They are quirks to be pointed out

"Meditation and Enactment" by Hugh Kenner. From *Poetry*, CII, No. 2 (May, 1963), 109–15. Copyright © 1963 by The Modern Poetry Association. Reprinted by permission of the author and the editor of *Poetry*.

on a calmer occasion, after the poem's main business, its scenario of exempla, has been received.

For such an occasion one would also reserve the question, why the third line ends in the middle of a word, especially as it may be difficult to know what to do with the answer. The answer is that the third line in each stanza has just 12 syllables. The syllabic patterning of a stanza, line by line, turns out to be 14, 8, 12, 16, 6, 20, 12, 6; and if the last line of stanza II has a syllable too few, the stanzaic average of 94 is exactly preserved by the fourth line of stanza III, which has one too many. This carefully idiosyncratic counting corresponds to the poet minding her own business without actually fussing to keep it a secret. It is also a piece of "conscious fastidiousness," to prevent the swan and the ant later in the poem, "ambition without understanding," from monopolizing that quality. This shades the poem's moral, which would otherwise have to align itself wholly with the intent primitivism of the child and the pup.

This poem is not measured like a picket-fence but grown like a crystal, its lattice of even-numbered members sustaining an equilibrium of little asymmetries. The words themselves, varying in weight and length, decorum and diction, press asymmetrically. The unit of symmetry, as in clavichord pieces, is the counted syllable, and the demonstration of symmetry is not the measure of a voice—which is occupied with enunciating highly irregular sentences—but the look of the page.

This look was badly obscured in the 1951 *Collected Poems,* where too narrow a printer's measure spoilt the visual neatness with frequent runover lines, and someone's notion of elegance treated the runover portions as though they were part of the stanza's scheme of indentation. It takes persistence to determine from that edition how many lines a stanza is supposed to have; in "The Plumet Basilisk," where the last line runs over misleadingly in every stanza but one, persistence is further impeded by a missing stanza-break (p. 26) and a dropped line (bottom of p. 28). The man whose characterization of her verse as "free" she quotes in mild mock-despair in her Foreword to the *Reader* had probably been misled by inspection of that 1951 volume. *Collected Poems* is a bad but not isolated example; only the 1921 *Poems* takes the sensible precaution of small enough type to accommodate most of her long lines without runovers. This matters, because the eye is supposed to tell us at once what kind of poems we are looking at.

A Marianne Moore Reader gave the printer a new chance with some of those long-familiar pieces. He has managed to reduce the number of runover lines, and had the tact to distinguish them by flush-right setting of the surplus portions. We can now read "Virginia Britannia" comfortably. But we cannot have a new look at "Critics and Connoisseurs": it is missing. So is "Camellia Sabina," so are "The

Plumet Basilisk" and "The Frigate Pelican"; so, all told, are 48 of the 71 *Collected Poems,* including the famous "Poetry," Miss Moore having perhaps grown tired of assuring questioners that, yes, she really does dislike it. The whole of the two later volumes, *Like a Bulwark* and *O To Be a Dragon,* plus five *Other Poems,* account for more than half the space the *Reader* allots to verse. (The rest, nearly two-thirds of the book, consists of a slim sampling of the La Fontaine, an interview with Donald Hall, and generous helpings of prose, some previously uncollected.) One trusts that *Reader* does mean *Sampler,* and not Miss Moore's final thoughts about the canon she has been revising for thirty years.

One trusts not, because few of the later poems *enact* as did so many of the earlier ones their lesson of probity. That enactment is their characteristic virtue; it is even entwined with their printing history, a record of delicate, minute decisions. *Nine Nectarines* and *Camellia Sabina* were slightly restructured between 1935 and 1951 to turn an internal rhyme into an end-rhyme, the first version having been judged perhaps a touch over-secretive. Whole blocks were sliced out of other poems. *The Steeple-Jack* is given in the *Reader* as "revised 1961." "Revised" means that 4½ stanzas that were present in 1935 but excised in 1951 are restored, slightly altered and amplified by yet one stanza more. This is tacit invitation to the curious student to pick his way through the three versions and decide why the cut was made in the first place. Since there was no attempt to conceal it—it left two stanzas of the rigid pattern broken—it became a gesture of fastidiousness. "There was once something here," said the broken stanzas, "that displeased me, and what is displeasing I will not reprint." What displeased her?

What pleases her? She has told us often enough, and summarizes in the *Reader*'s foreword: "straight writing, end-stopped lines, an effect of flowing continuity"; also matter not manner, substance not shadow, rapture not ego; also "animals and athletes," because "They are subjects for art and exemplars of it, are they not? minding their own business. Pangolins, hornbills, pitchers, catchers, do not pry or prey— or prolong the conversation; do not make us self-conscious; look their best in caring least. . . ." They teach us, in short, how to enact virtue in concealing our art, *by* concealing it. It is often a prodigious art that Miss Moore conceals. Take "Bird-Witted":

> With innocent wide penguin eyes, three
>   large fledgling mocking-birds below
> the pussy-willow tree,
>   stand in a row,
> wings touching, feebly solemn,
> till they see

            their no longer larger
            mother bringing
       something which will partially
       feed one of them.

They are calling, "ee," "ee," "ee"; and when mother arrives, toward the end of this single sentence as precariously balanced on its principal verb as the three young birds, their cry is muted to the final syllable of "partially." Then, food now in sight, the chorus is raised with new urgency:

      Toward the high-keyed intermittent squeak
        of broken carriage-springs, made by
      the three similar, meek-
        coated bird's-eye-
      freckled forms she comes; and when
      from the beak
        of one, the still living
        beetle has dropped
      out, she picks it up and puts
      it in again.

"Eak," "eek," "eak"; it sounds when our attention is on them, stops when we are attending to the mother; and there is affectionate mimesis in the awkward "dropped / out" and the businesslike

          she picks it up and puts
        it in again.

The birds have their own business to attend to, and their business is not with Miss Moore's end-stopped line. Her lines can however recall, without apparent effort, the song of the grown bird too, as if to assure us that the poem's compass is not confined, like the birds at this moment, to grotesque kinetic miniature:

      . . . What delightful note
        with rapid unexpected flute-
      sounds leaping from the throat
        of the astute
      grown bird, comes back to one from
      the remote
        unenergetic sun-
        lit air before
      the brood was here? How harsh
      the bird's voice has become.

The song in "ute" and "ote" echoes without effort, and drops into harshness at the very moment when a flat little terminal sentence ekes out the run of the stanza. No poem is more careful of its sounds, of husbanding its effects and expending them at an exact moment, or of adjusting and readjusting syntax to pattern, crowding, for instance, portions of a sentence onto precipitous little lines as (see Stanza V) the small birds test their footing. It is a very great feat. Pound had praised Arnaut Daniel in the *ABC of Reading* (1934) for making the birds sing "IN HIS WORDS," and then repeating the strophic pattern over and over, "WITH the words making sense." Miss Moore's poem first appeared in 1935, perhaps in response to this praise; it brings to Daniel's tradition of the musical irregular stanza her own particularities of observation, not only of how creatures look but of how they perform actions, not like machines but like intent systems of attention; and in being worthy to stand beside Daniel's (who was Dante's *miglior fabbro*) it provides not a medieval pastiche but a measure of the difference between 1935 and 1190. Arnaut's birds are emblems, of spring in the year and in the heart; Miss Moore's squeal, shuffle, miss their footing, on the tree, in the mind, in the poem, observed with the minute participating patience of an Agassiz.

And the moral enactment? It is in the scrupulous care for what the birds are doing, no nuance of presentation sacrificed to pattern despite that inexorable counting of syllables. This moral rises to explicit drama at the end, with the discomfiture of

> the
> intellectual cautious-
> ly creeping cat,

which the vigilant mother, "with bayonet beak and cruel wings," "half kills." For the cat, "intellectual," birds are to eat: to us: to appropriate into his own legato sleekness. If the bird turns "cruel," it is to preserve its autonomous identity, exactly as this poem has allowed it to do for six stanzas. The shape of the poem has not at any time crowded it, nor oppressed it, nor reduced it to cliché, nor even pretended, for the sake of melody, that its voice has not become "harsh." And yet the poem has preserved its own identity too, just 54 syllables per stanza, flawlessly divided, 9, 8, 6, 4, 7, 3, 6, 4, 7, 4.

One might sort Miss Moore's poems into those that observe, meditate, and enact in this way, the rigorous pattern a dimension of meditation and enactment; those that soliloquize, like "A Grave" or "New York," and have as their center of gravity therefore the speaker's probity and occasional tartness; and those (rather frequent of late) that incite, that set themselves to *exact,* appropriate feelings about something public. For her public occasions Miss Moore seems a little dependent on the newspapers; "Carnegie Hall: Rescued" has her inimitable texture, but the sentiment of the poem is extrinsic to that texture. The sentiment is that of *The New York Times* and *The*

New Yorker, public relief, public gratitude; yes, public platitude. One need not quarrel with the sentiments to find the poems dedicated to them unlucky. The poems simply participate, with busy flutter and stir of unexpected particulars, in what right-thinking people would, presumably, think without their aid. And the fastidiousness that chopped whole sequences of stanzas out of "The Steeple-Jack" and "The Frigate Pelican" and "Nine Nectarines" because irritated by minute inadequacies is now willing out of public spirit to glue mannerism over cliché:

> rescuer of a music hall
> menaced by the "cannibal
>   of real estate"—bulldozing potentate,
>   land-grabber, the human crab
>   left cowering like a neonate.

Mannerism, agreeable mannerism, is what the newcomer is likely to suppose Miss Moore chiefly offers, if the *Reader* is to be his introduction. A manner offers pleasures of its own; but whether a reader so introduced is likely to notice, when he turns back to "The Buffalo" or "The Pangolin," anything but the idiosyncratically close observation, set into an unaccountably rigorous stanza, is open to question. Such poems were receiving too casual an attention even before *The New Yorker,* by developing Miss Moore as a "personality," left everyone with so misleading a clue.

Meanwhile the former work stands, deferred to but seldom explored. Critical curiosity, which has fussed over so many twentieth century pages, has tended to leave Miss Moore's poems approvingly uninvestigated. If she is now able to take for granted some of the lessons in her own early work, there is no reason why anyone else should. She has had the discipline of doing the work; we have hardly begun to know what it means to read it. And if some of the late writing tends to encourage criticism in its tacit abandonment of her reputation to the keeping of the *Harper's Bazaar* and *New Yorker* publics, it is criticism—articulate understanding—that loses. She is not merely idiosyncratic; not merely uniquely herself; she is much more than "the greatest living observer." Counting her syllables, revealing and concealing her rhymes, setting down her finely particularized exempla for elucidation by tone alone, putting "unconscious elegance" into tension against "sophistication" and showing how art, a third thing, can endorse the former without false entanglement in the latter, she has accomplished things of general import to the maintenance of language that no one else has had the patience, the skill, the discipline, or the perfect unselfconscious conviction to adumbrate.

The Proper Plenitude of Fact[1]

by Denis Donoghue

Miss Moore's first book was called, simply, *Poems*. Her second was *Observations*. The titles are interchangeable. "I like to describe things," she remarks in "Subject, Predicate, Object," an aesthetic given in three modest pages of *Tell Me, Tell Me*. Her favourite mood is the indicative, pointing to things. Optatives are rare; imperatives are normally addressed to herself. The pleasure of writing a poem, she has said, is "consolation, rapture, to be achieving a likeness of the thing visualized." Poetry is a way of looking, various because vision is irregular, reasonable because, irregular, it is not indiscriminate. Yeats distinguished between the glance and the gaze, and William Empson took care to discover what a man sees through the corner of the eye. The distinction between appearance and reality is not to Miss Moore a cause of persistent distress. To think appearance significant is not a mark of folly; it is a mode of appreciation, or predilection. Things may be deceptive, but a relation between one thing and another is something achieved. So it is good to look at things, observing.

Mostly, the observations in Miss Moore are her own; of plants, animals, birds, the giraffe, the pangolin, clocks, baseball, jewels. But this poet, gorgeous in observation, is the first to acknowledge that someone else has been observant. "Blue Bug" started from a photograph by Thomas McAvoy in *Sports Illustrated*; of eight polo ponies, one of them like a dancer or the acrobat Li Siau Than. "The Arctic Ox" was set astir by an essay in the *Atlantic Monthly*, the essayist John J. Teal, who rears musk oxen on his farm in Vermont. A recent poem praises Leonardo da Vinci, impassioned calligrapher of flower, acorns, and rocks. The hero of "Granite and Steel" is John Roebling, praised for inventing Roebling cable. Throughout her poems Miss Moore is on hand to defend the rights of "small ingenuities," keeping

From "The Proper Plenitude of Fact" by Denis Donoghue. From *The Ordinary Universe* (London: Faber & Faber, Ltd.; New York: The Macmillan Co., 1968). Reprinted by permission of the author and publishers.

[1] "Fact / has its proper plenitude / that only time and tact / will show, renew." (See Charles Tomlinson, *A Peopled Landscape*, Oxford, 1963, p. 14.)

open the "eye of the mind." Gracious, she delights in grace, skill, gusto, charity, the rescue of Carnegie Hall, the "enfranchising cable" of Brooklyn Bridge.

So Miss Moore's poems are poetic as natural science is poetic; botany, meteorology. Some years ago she defended the comparison of poet and scientist. "Both are willing to waste effort. To be hard on himself is one of the main strengths of each. Each is attentive to clues, each must narrow the choice, must strive for precision." In "The Staff of Aesculapius" she writes in praise of cancer research, virology, knowledge "gained for another attack" upon suffering. There are several poems in defence of experimental waste. Anything is poetic, Miss Moore implies, conducted in the proper spirit of disinterestedness and charity. A poet writes a poem, perhaps, to revive a root meaning long buried. The reader consults a large dictionary, finds the old meaning, and recognizes it, revived, in its new setting. These are poetic acts, honourably wasteful. One of Miss Moore's favourite writers is Christopher Smart, author of "Jubilate Agno." Another is Landor, praised in a recent poem, who could throw a man through a window and yet say, 'Good God, the violets!' Miss Moore loves dapple, dappled things, the evidence of spirited acts. She does not like a big splash. She likes circumstance, released from pomp. She thinks Caesar a great writer and Defoe observant to the degree of genius.

"Accessibility to experience" is Henry James's phrase, invoked for admiration in Miss Moore's poem "New York" and elsewhere recalled in prose. It is reasonable to say that this is Miss Moore's way of being an American, like James in this respect a characteristic American. When she quotes a sentence from James's study of Hawthorne, its light returns upon herself. Hawthorne was dear to James because he "proved to what a use American matter could be put by an American hand." An American "could be an artist, one of the finest, without 'going outside'; quite, in fact, as if Hawthorne had become one just by being American enough." We think of Williams in Rutherford, Stevens in Hartford, Miss Moore in Manhattan. "The Gods of China are always Chinese," Stevens said. Miss Moore likes to quote from James the advice to Christopher Newman: "Don't try to be anyone else"; and if triumph comes, "let it then be all you." But she does not endorse a predatory grasp of reality. Instead, she is the first to concede to a thing its own independent right; an acknowledgement rather than a concession. In her colony of the spirit there are no chain gangs. It does not gratify her to bring things to heel, seeing them cower. She is a poet of finite things; she does not lust for the absolute. She is always patient in the presence of limitation. A recent poem, "Charity overcoming Envy," says: "The Gordian knot need not be cut."

Of eternal things in this poetry there is little to be said. Miss Moore has her own sense of them, but it is private. She praises Landor for a corresponding reticence; who, considering infinity and eternity, would only say: "I'll talk about them when I understand them." Miss Moore does not claim to understand everything; not even everything she sees. She speaks when, observant, she has something to report. She is no mystic. This is the measure of her care for things, relationship, words; a care habitually engaged in accuracy. Quoting Martin Buber: "The free man believes in destiny and that it has need of him"; she adds, "Destiny, not fate." A sentence culled from James's *Notes of a Son and Brother* is to her "an instance of reverent, and almost reverend, feeling that would defend him against the charge of casualness in anything, if ever one were inclined to make it." Miss Moore's poems are full of quotations because she has come upon many things which have only to be exhibited to be appreciated, and appreciation is poetic. One thing, placed beside another, if both are judiciously chosen, sets a new relation in train. The main duty is to get the words right. This is why Miss Moore is stern in revising her poems.

So the revisions are always instructive. Usually they are the result, she says, of "impatience with unkempt diction and lapses in logic, together with an awareness that for most defects, to delete is the instantaneous cure." Sometimes the change is designed to strengthen the syntax, where the burden is excessive. In *Tell Me, Tell Me* the poem "Sun" is revised. An earlier version included the lines:

> O Sun, you shall stay
> with us. Holiday
> and day of wrath shall be one,
> wound in a device
> of Moorish gorgeousness,
> round glasses spun
> to flame hemispheres of one
> great hour-glass dwindling to a stem.[2]

The internal rhymes are gay, but perhaps they are too much, gaudy. The repetition of "one," if not unkempt, is loose. But the author of "The Pangolin" would not wish to delete the invocation to the sun, "that comes into and steadies my soul," so she tidies the diction by eliminating the repetition, letting the rest stand:

> O Sun, you shall stay
> with us; holiday,
> consuming wrath, be wound in a device
> of Moorish gorgeousness, round glasses spun

[2] *A Marianne Moore Reader* (New York: Viking Press, 1961), p. 88.

> to flame as hemispheres of one
> great hour-glass dwindling to a stem.[3]

The relation between the holiday and the wrath is changed, but the new relation is more in keeping with the urgency of the prayer. Miss Moore cares for these things, her small ingenuities. She likes to recite the fable of La Fontaine about the song that preserved the life of the swan mistaken by the cook for a goose; the moral of the story being, "Sweet speech does no harm—none at all." Admiring "an elegance of which the source is not bravado," she writes as if every poem were a swansong, sweet but not lugubrious. There are things a swan may not do, even to save her life. Many of the poems are the result of stitching and unstitching, but they sound like "a moment's thought" (Yeats's test in "Adam's Curse"). Some of them, speech after long silence, have that fatality of cadence which is Miss Moore's trademark:

> You understand terror, know how
>   to deal
> with pent-up emotion, a ballad,
>   witchcraft.
> I don't. O Zeus and O Destiny!

But these cadences are not, as we say, "merely verbal," they are a form of good manners, "values in use." Miss Moore's poems have the kind of grace, civility, and candor which we find in English verse epistles of the sixteenth and seventeenth centuries. When her lines are unforgettable, it is not because "in the accepted sense" they do things "in a big way"; it is because they are true, genuine, and because they have that "tame excitement" on which she thrives. The objective is "fertile procedure." In a recent poem Envy is delineated:

> Envy, on a dog, is worn down by
>   obsession,
> his greed (since of things owned by
>   others
> he can only take *some*).

Things well done are "inventions with wing."

So the relation between Miss Moore and the language she uses is remarkably intimate. She can do more with abstractions than any modern poet, Eliot excepted: reticence, propriety, mobility, probity, deference, magnanimity. Her favourite word, I guess from internal evidence, is ardour, in French and English: "*Sentir avec ardeur:* with fire; yes, with passion." Her favourite image, by the same guess, is the kite. "With no resistance, a kite staggers and falls; whereas if it catches the right current of air it can rise, darting and soaring as it pulls and

---

[3] Marianne Moore, *Tell Me, Tell Me* (New York: Viking Press, 1967), p. 49.

fights the wind." Hence "the mind is an enchanting thing," and poetry is "the Mogul's dream: to be intensively toiling at what is a pleasure."

So, thinking of Miss Moore's poems in general before looking at one of them in particular, we think of activities at once work and play; or things like ice-skating which are hard play. The function of a poem, when Miss Moore writes it, is to provide for distinctive energy of mind a sufficient occasion; a direction. The mind moves from its presumed rest; ranges abroad through materials congenial to its nature; comes to rest again. This is the figure the poems make; a sequence, a curve, the trajectory of a mind well aimed. If we ask why one curve is chosen in preference to another, there is no ready answer: it is so. The assumption is that energy of mind is good, and its release in action is good. The note is experimental, exploratory. . . .

"The Pangolin" is a celebration of difference, of the benign force which makes a thing what it is and keeps it in that state. The first stanzas disengage the pangolin from any human use, invasion of its privacy: observation guarantees this. Gertrude Stein said that "description is evaluation," an admonition congenial to Miss Moore, who is content to have the evaluation reside silently in descriptions almost scientific. Once the pangolin is safe in its own nature, the poet can afford to let the mind roam a little:

> Pangolins are not aggressive animals; between
> dusk and day they have the measured
> tread of the machine—
> the slow frictionless creep of a thing
> made graceful by adversities, con-
>
> versities. To explain grace requires
> a curious hand. If that which is at all were not forever,
> why would those who graced the spires
> with animals and gathered there to rest, on cold luxurious
> low stone seats—a monk and monk and monk—between
> the thus
> ingenious roof-supports, have slaved to confuse
> grace with a kindly manner, time in which to
> pay a debt
> the cure for sins, a graceful use
> of what are yet
> approved stone mullions branching out
> across
> the perpendiculars? A sailboat
>
> was the first machine.[4]

---

[4] *A Marianne Moore Reader, supra,* p. 38. The text of this passage differs somewhat from that in *Collected Poems* (New York: Macmillan, 1952), p. 120.

I have quoted the final version, somewhat tidied in diction between 1951 and 1961. We assume that Miss Moore came upon the first "graceful" in the ordinary way, since it is a word near at hand and natural. The first event of distinctive imagination is the jump from "adversities" to "conversities." "Adversities" is moral in its first meaning, since the Latin is dead there, until it is restored to figurative life by the recognition of the Latin in "conversities." The poet does not spurn an extensive meaning even if it comes by linguistic chance. The effect is to light up both words; and then to throw this double light back upon "graceful." So the next passage is derived from this happy chance. "To explain grace requires a curious hand." Already the word is moving buoyantly between a spiritual and a secular meaning. "Curious," meaning now "careful," because Latin is in the air. "Hand," because the true explanation is to do it: no explanation but in action. "If that which is at all were not forever"; a variant of Yeats's "All lives that has lived"; just as one word, "grace," serves two or several masters, natural and supernatural, so anything that exists is, in a sense, eternally existent. The next lines are a lively illustration of the fact that, as Miss Moore says in "The Sycamore," "there's more than just one kind of grace." To set an animal upon a spire is to bring the several worlds together, honouring all. The monks are the appropriate adepts, graceful in two worlds. Miss Moore's monks live at once in both worlds, not painfully divided and distinguished but genial. Hence they have slaved to confuse grace (supernatural) with its several human forms, social, legal, ecclesiastical, architectural. These are various enough to stand for all the other forms, unspecified. The basic pattern of the verse, then, is the observation, followed by an elucidation sufficient to make the observation shine; text and gloss. The nature of grace is enlivened by sentences involving "graceful," "graced," and so on. I. A. Richards once set the opening lines of Donne's "First Anniversary" beside Dryden's "Ode to Mrs. Anne Killigrew; the point being that in Donne's verse "there is a prodigious activity between the words as we read them." [5] Following, exploring, understanding Donne's words is not a preparation for reading the poem: "it is itself the poem." In Dryden, on the other hand, "the words are in routine conventional relations like peaceful diplomatic communications between nations." Dryden's words "do not induce revolutions in one another and are not thereby attempting to form a new order." Can we not say, allowing for the differences, that in "The Pangolin" the activity between the words as we read them is great, if not prodigious? The words, as we cope with them, are forming new relations in our minds; or, what is often the same thing, breaking up dead relations already entombed there. The verse is purifying "the

[5] Reprinted in Irving Howe (editor), *Modern Literary Criticism* (New York: Grove Press, 1958), pp. 85 foll.

dialect of the tribe" by sending an imaginative force to range through tribal words. Think, to illustrate again, what "luxurious" does to "cold low stone seats," otherwise conventional enough: it sets the common phrase stirring from within.

So the question to ask about a poem by Marianne Moore is not: what are all these details doing here?; but rather, what, given these details, is the principle of their relation? The ethic of Miss Moore's verse implies that if we treat objects as objects, rather than as functions of ourselves, and if we send the mind to explore them in their own terms, the encounter of subject and object is likely to be rewarding. If the spaces of life are occupied by generous perception, there is less room for nasty things; belligerence, bravado, cruelty, condescension. No other poet writes like Miss Moore: not even William Carlos Williams, who learned from her how lightly a poet may travel. The reason is partly the choice of objects; and about this there is nothing useful to be said, except that the choice is personal and intimate. "The Pangolin," for instance, begins *de facto* and ends *de jure.* Her preoccupation: the personal and moral possibilities of *ici-bas,* despite everything.

Two Philologists

by Henry Gifford

A woman poet who is also American will find herself measured sooner or later against Emily Dickinson. Few of them may like this, because the comparison will seem invidious on two grounds. Why should women be judged as poets differently from men? And is it fair that competition should be set so high? Emily Dickinson was, at her best, a poet unequalled in American literature. We may admit the complaint and still proceed with the experiment. After all, our great women novelists have certain virtues in common that seem to derive from their situation as female writers: a sense of mundane realities; a severity and firmness that are not accompanied, like the severity and firmness of Wordsworth for example, by a veneration for oneself; a directness and ease in writing—particularly about everyday things— to attain the like of which men writers have to unromanticize their minds and undergo a long course of self-discipline. The same qualities are to be seen in women poets—an Emily Dickinson or an Emily Brontë—who even in their most passionate moments never cease to be "literalists of the imagination." In judging a woman poet, then, we think first of the poet, but expect that her endowments as a woman will in certain ways modify what she writes. The poetry when it most succeeds will be recognizable like all good poetry; if unusually honest, not more so than the best poetry of men; if exceptionally lucid, that too is a sign by which we know poetry anywhere. No such thing exists as a female tradition in poetry; but there are feminine attributes which a woman poet cannot overlook in herself without falsity.

Marianne Moore and Emily Dickinson do not stand to each other in a relationship as undeniable as that between Miss Moore and Henry James. I doubt if one who had mastered the urbane obliquity of James would care altogether for the abrupt and unceremonious withdrawals into enigma of Emily Dickinson. It has often been re-marked that Marianne Moore's style develops out of highly civilised prose. Her sentences are beautifully articulated, more condensed than

"Two Philologists" by Henry Gifford. This essay is published here for the first time. Copyright © 1969 by Henry Gifford.

prose normally is, and with an odd sidelong movement that in prose would probably disconcert; but no one could mistake the element from which they have arisen. Their affinities are with conversation—

> I, too, dislike it. . . .
>
> I remember a swan under the willows in Oxford. . . .
>
> This man said—I think that I repeat
> his identical words:
> 'Hebrew poetry is
> prose with a sort of heightened consciousness.' . . .

That last phrase suggests what kind of conversation her poetry has in view. It calls for the hearer to participate: the "heightened consciousness" is nothing if not shared—a discovery in their conversation. Emily Dickinson was afraid to converse: she utters a few astonishing words from behind the door and then closes it in palpitation. She too wants her "heightened consciousness" to find its response—but from whom? Higginson? Wadsworth? Her sister-in-law? or Helen Hunt Jackson? All were obtuse in their degree. It is more likely that she resembled Osip Mandelstam in writing for the ideal "interlocutor," who at the appointed time and place would decipher the message sealed in a bottle and cast on the sea. Emily Dickinson all but abolished prose from her written communications with the world. Any letter might turn into a poem, the main difference being that a letter used the same devices but these were scaled down to the abilities of the recipient.

And yet, given this all-important distinction between the two poets, their choice of language seems to unite them unexpectedly. Both are incontrovertibly American—or perhaps one should say American of a certain tone and temper which, like much else in the modern world, may be dissolving. They are individual, ironic, and above all fastidious. They place a high value on privacy and know the power of reticence. Their poetry is exact and curious like the domestic skills of the American woman in ante-bellum days. It has the elevation of old-fashioned erudite American talk—more careful in its vocabulary, more strenuously aiming at correctness and dignity than English talk of the same vintage. This is not to confuse the milieux of Emily Dickinson and Marianne Moore; nor to insinuate that both poets stand at a distance from today in a charming lady-like quaintness. What distinguishes them is something very far from quaintness: a practical interest in the capacities of the English language both learned and colloquial, in its American variety.

The point has to be made—though it is by now familiar—that American speech (in the pre-Hemingway era) showed an almost Scottish partiality for Latinized diction. At its not infrequent worst

this was chronic Micawberism; but it could allow, when properly
used, for a greatly increased range of tone and for delicate discrimina-
tions. Emily Dickinson was less singular in her readiness to employ
such a vocabulary than in her subversive use of it. She had the hardi-
hood to restore all the meanings in a Latin-derived word and to play
one off against another. She often ventures a critique of the theological
language still in possession at Amherst by framing it to her own
startling and heretical insights. She knew how to exploit, as Allen
Tate and others have remarked, the two opposing elements of our
vocabulary—"the Latin for ideas and the Saxon for perceptions."
She and Hopkins were the two aptest pupils of Shakespeare in her
time, but Hopkins never learned, as she did, to extract from the
Latin its full value. English poetry through the nineteenth century
down to the Georgians would seem to have grown more and more
shy of Latin. By any reckoning, the ideas of William Barnes are
eccentric; but it would not, I think, have occurred to an American
exponent of the rural life that Saxon words are necessarily more
wholesome than Latin. When Thoreau went to the woods he did
not leave his Latin vocabulary behind in Concord.

Through Emily Dickinson's latinizing one hears continually the
accents of her New England speech. This attention to the living idiom
around her shows in more than the choice of a dialect word like *heft*
or the use of *some* as an adverb. It is manifest in a tone—casual and
terse—which belongs to her own New England milieu. And certain
poems avoid Latinate diction altogether—for instance

> The Wind begun to knead the Grass—
> As Women do a Dough—
> He flung a Hand full at the Plain—
> A Hand full at the Sky—
> The Leaves unhooked themselves from Trees—
> And started all abroad—
> The Dust did scoop itself like Hands—
> And throw away the Road. . . .

This, and practically every word in the poem as it continues, would
have satisfied William Barnes, though he would not have approved
the change from "Hand full" to "Menace" in the second version.
(And noting the substitution, we may ask whether Allen Tate could
say here, at least, that Latin is not for sensations.) Perhaps the last four
lines quoted above, in their strange and violent humor, could only
have been written by an American poet.

Marianne Moore too has the keenest appreciation of the vernacular,
though as she told Donald Hall it scarcely shows in her verse. This
may be so partly because she lacks the support of a close community
like Amherst in Emily Dickinson's day. The little town of Marianne

Moore's "The Steeple-Jack" is a town (whatever its actuality outside the poem) which exists in a picture-frame:

> Dürer would have seen a reason for living
> in a town like this. . . .

Emily Dickinson's funeral visitants ("There's been a Death, in the Opposite House"), Doctor, Minister, Milliner,

> and the Man
> Of the Appalling Trade—,

have an actuality denied to C. J. Poole, Steeple-Jack, though his solicitude may be touching and real. Similarly, when Miss Moore speaks of "my father" who understood the restraint of superior people and the limits of hospitality, she has invented this parent. Edward Dickinson would have brooked no surrogates: the pressure of Amherst was something often resented by his daughter but unremovable. Its life went on "in the Opposite House." For poets since her time the mutuality, the fixity of relationship implied in that phrase, have largely gone. Miss Moore's Americanism had to be gathered from the language itself, one feels, rather than from any single community.

It is here that she meets Emily Dickinson, who looked out on to the street and as often turned back to her "Lexicon." Marianne Moore does not accept the direction of words or regard them with the same religious awe as Emily Dickinson:

> A Word made Flesh is seldom
> And tremblingly partook. . . .

But in a more detached way she loves to see words about their job; and she follows Emily Dickinson in her concern with "philology."

When Eliot wrote an introduction to Miss Moore's *Selected Poems* of 1935, he particularly praised the service they had done to the language.[1] Increasingly we look to the poet in these days not only to maintain the subtleties of language but to save human nature from shrinking into a gradual incapacitation for "felt life." Marianne Moore has devised a complex and refined medium to express her own sensibility; and the poets of the English-speaking world have much to learn from it. Hers is a wholly individual voice, yet not, like the voice of Stevens or indeed Yeats, conscious at every moment of its uniqueness. The apprenticeship to prose has made her achievements more communicable than theirs.

A characteristic poem by Marianne Moore hovers between the colloquial and the instructed, just as it embodies her own spontaneous thoughts and a mass of felicitous quotation. The tone is equable and gracious, but never intimate: Miss Moore holds herself at a distance.

---

[1] [See T. S. Eliot's "Introduction to *Selected Poems*" above, pp. 60–65.]

The "I" in her poems is not central and exposed like the "I" in Emily Dickinson's. Rather it appears when comment is needed, or to provide a focus:

> I recall their magnificence, now not more magnificent
> than it is dim. It is difficult to recall the ornament,
>   speech, and precise manner of what one might
>   call the minor acquaintances twenty
>   years back. . . .

Almost at once the personal becomes generalized: "it is difficult. . . ." And her bent for anthologizing, for grafting quotations on to the living stock of her poem, leads also to a tactful self-effacement, for the sake of showing whatever it may be more clearly. Marianne Moore inhabits her poetry as a watchful commentator, much as Jane Austen can be sensed in every line of her novels. The actual incidence of the first person is not to the point. What reveals her throughout is a consistent tone.

The tone derives its authority from a philologist's care:

> This institution,
> perhaps one should say enterprise
> out of respect for which
> one says one need not change one's mind
> about a thing one has believed in,
> requiring public promises
> of one's intention
> to fulfil a private obligation:
> I wonder what Adam and Eve
> think of it by this time,
> this fire-gilt steel
> alive with goldenness—
> how bright it shows. . . .
>
>   ("Marriage")

The words have no surprising depths, as they would in Emily Dickinson; but the public forms, as with her, the institution or enterprise, the obligation, are weighted against the private feelings—

> alive with goldenness—
> how bright it shows. . . .

and the Latin words, by being thus scrutinized in face of living experience, take on their full meaning—*obligation,* for instance, later in the poem is glossed unobtrusively as "bondage." Everywhere, she actualizes her abstract terms, which may be quotations, by doing what Emily Dickinson did—exposing them to the world of sensation. "It is not," she declares of New York,

> . . . that estimated in raw meat and berries,
>   we could feed the universe;
>   it is not the atmosphere of ingenuity,
>   the otter, the beaver, the puma-skins
>   without shooting-irons or dogs;
>   it is not the plunder,
>   but 'accessibility to experience'.

The last phrase was indisputably alive to its originator, Henry James; but it acquires here, after the mention of "raw meat and berries," "shooting-irons"—rifles as the victim might see them—and "dogs," a specific weight and impressiveness of its own.

One could examine poem after poem to reiterate the proof. Marianne Moore's work houses a museumful of detail, drawn from her own observation, from her reading in such books as *Strange Animals I have Known,* from art galleries, and from *The Illustrated London News.* She has assembled all these objects and impressions for the imagination to work into a new arrangement. So with language, the specimens of its use for a myriad purposes are presently given their place in a poem. Entering they are changed, it may be in almost imperceptible ways. The English language with all its Latin accretions is perhaps more than any other prone to degeneracy. It has to be kept alive from one era to the next, as indeed do all languages; and the most effective way with ours is that of Emily Dickinson and Marianne Moore—to restore the Latin words to their full rights by engaging them in the common labour of interpreting and assaying experience. They serve mostly to balance and control—or, adopting a favorite mode of Emily Dickinson's, to *adjust* or *regulate:*

> And then an awful leisure was
> Belief to regulate

—where again the notion is tested against the shock of experience.

Marianne Moore's emotional pitch and range differ from those of Emily Dickinson. They do not exclude terror: the

> moment of danger that lays on heart and lungs the
> weight of the python that crushes to powder

or ecstasy:

> Below the incandescent stars
> below the incandescent fruit,
> the strange experience of beauty

which turns into something destructive like terror:

> its existence is too much;
> it tears one to pieces

> and each fresh wave of consciousness
> is poison.

But these notes are not habitual. Her attitude usually is that of the alert spectator, as indeed in the poem "Marriage," from which I have just quoted. Her essential kinship with Emily Dickinson can be explained partly by the obvious facts that they are both women poets and both American; but it would scarcely add to our understanding of either did we not recognize the common bond of philology. To probe meanings, to read the past history and the present possibilities of words, to modify them by an apt new employment, to keep them adventurous and generative—such has always been the concern of the poet. Marianne Moore and Emily Dickinson have their separate ways of bringing words into prominence, and this essay could enlarge on the emphasis given by Emily Dickinson's dissonant rhymes, and the manner in which Marianne Moore's light rhymes duck to make way for the stress where it is most needed. But the important thing was to signalize what is common to their achievement, and to express gratitude for what they have done.

Marianne (Craig) Moore: A Brief Chronology

by Richard A. Macksey

. . . Even so, "deference"; yes, deference may be my defense.

1887	November 15: born in Kirkwood, a suburb of St. Louis, Missouri; daughter of John Milton and Mary (Warner) Moore; her father, an engineer, suffers a nervous breakdown after the failure of his plans to manufacture a smokeless furnace and returns to his parents' home in Portsmouth, Ohio; Mrs. Moore moves the family to the home of her father, the Reverend John Riddle Warner, pastor of the Kirkwood Presbyterian Church.
1894	Following the death of Reverend Warner, the family moves to Carlisle, Pennsylvania.
1896	Begins preparatory education at Metzger Institute, Carlisle.
1905	Enters Bryn Mawr College. (Hilda Doolittle is among her fellow students.)
1909	A.B. from Bryn Mawr.
1910	Graduates from Carlisle Commercial College.
1911	Spends a summer traveling in England and France.
1911–15	Teaches "commercial subjects" at the United States Indian School in Carlisle. (Jim Thorpe is one of her students.)
1915	First publishes in *The Egoist* (May) and later contributes to *Poetry*.
1916	Moves with her mother to Chatham, New Jersey, to keep house for her brother John, assigned there as a Presbyterian minister.
1918	After her brother joins the Navy as a chaplain, she moves with her mother to an apartment on St. Luke's Place in Greenwich Village; brief employment as a secretary in a girl's school and as a private tutor. The beginning of her friendships with poets of Alfred Kreymborg's *Others* group, including William Carlos Williams, Wallace Stevens, Kenneth Burke, and Conrad Aiken.
1920	Her work begins to appear in the recently "re-established" little magazine supported by Scofield Thayer and Dr. J. S. Watson, *The Dial*.
1921–25	Serves as an assistant at the Hudson Park branch of The New York Public Library.
1921	*Poems*. London: Egoist Press. (Published without the author's knowledge at the instigation of H. D. and Bryher.)

"Marianne (Craig) Moore: A Brief Chronology." Prepared for this volume by Richard A. Macksey. Copyright © 1969 by Richard A. Macksey.

1923   "Marriage" published separately. Mannikin #3, Monroe Wheeler.

1924   *Observations.* New York: The Dial Press. (Reprint with additions of the London *Poems.*) Receives the Dial Award for 1924.

1925   Becomes acting editor of *The Dial* beginning with the July issue; her time is increasingly occupied with editing.

1926   Assumes the full editorship of *The Dial.*

1929   July: the last issue of *The Dial* appears; moves with her mother from Greenwich Village to Brooklyn (Cumberland Street) in order to be closer to her brother John, now assigned to the Navy Yard.

1932   Helen Haire Levinson Prize for Poetry.

1935   *Selected Poems.* New York: Macmillan. Ernest Hartsock Memorial Prize. *Selected Poems.* London: Faber & Faber, Ltd. With an introduction by T. S. Eliot.

1936   *The Pangolin and other verse.* London: Bredin Publishing Co. (Five poems published in an edition of 120 copies.)

1940   Shelley Memorial Award.

1941   *What Are Years?* New York: Macmillan.

1942   Teaches composition at the Cummington School.

1944   *Nevertheless.* New York: Macmillan. Contemporary Poetry's Patrons' Prize; Harriet Monroe Poetry Award.

1945   Guggenheim Fellowship. Translates, with Elizabeth Mayer, *Rock Crystal, A Christmas Tale* by Adalbert Stifter.

1946   Joint grant from American Academy of Arts and Letters and National Institute of Arts and Letters.

1947   Death of Mrs. Moore. Elected to National Institute of Arts and Letters.

1949   "A Face" published separately. Cummington Press.

1951   *Collected Poems.* New York: Macmillan. Work receives the Pulitzer Prize for poetry, National Book Award, and Bollingen Prize (1953).

1953   Visiting Lecturer at Bryn Mawr; receives the M. Carey Thomas Award and National Institute of Arts and Letters Gold Medal.

1954   Translates *The Fables of La Fontaine.* New York: Viking. *Gedichte,* a bilingual edition of poems, published in Germany.

1955   *Predilections.* New York: Viking. (Selected essays.) *Selected Fables of La Fontaine.* London: Faber & Faber, Ltd.

1956   *Like a Bulwark.* New York: Viking.

1957   Participates in the First Bollingen Poetry Festival at The Johns Hopkins University. *Letters from and to the Ford Motor Company* (concerning the selection of a name for the automobile finally called "Edsel"). New York: Pierpont Morgan Library. (Reprinted from *New Yorker,* April 13, 1957.)

1958   Edits *Riverside Poetry Three: An Anthology of Student Poetry.* New York: Twayne. *Idiosyncracy and Technique: Two Lectures.* Berkeley: University of California Press.

1959   *O to Be a Dragon.* New York: Viking. *A Marianne Moore Reader.* New York: Viking. Contributes to *Four Poets on Poetry.* Baltimore: The Johns Hopkins Press.

1962   *The Absentee: A Comedy in Four Acts.* New York: House of Books. (Based on Maria Edgeworth's novel of the same title.)

1963   Translates and adapts three tales by Charles Perrault: *Puss in Boots, The Sleeping Beauty, and Cinderella.* New York: Macmillan. "The Giraffe" in *Poetry in Crystal.* New York: Steuben Glass Co.

1964   *The Arctic Ox.* London: Faber and Faber. *Festschrift for Marianne Moore's Seventy-Seventh Birthday* edited by T. Tambimuttu. New York: Tambimuttu and Mass.

1965   Laurence Scott at the Ibex Press, Cambridge, Mass., prints a number of ephemeral items coincident with the poet's visit to Harvard in the spring: *Dress and Kindred Subjects; Le Mariage,* translated by Jeffrey Kindley; *Silence; A Talisman.* Her replies to questions by Howard Nemerov are published as *Poetry and Criticism* by the Adams House and Lowell House Printers. Returns to Manhattan.

1966   *Tell Me, Tell Me: Granite, Steel, and Other Topics.* New York: Viking.

1967   *The Complete Poems of Marianne Moore.* New York: Viking and Macmillan.

Notes on the Editor and Contributors

CHARLES TOMLINSON, poet and critic, is Reader in English Poetry at the University of Bristol. Among other books of verse, he has published *Seeing is Believing* and *American Scenes*.

ROBERT BELOOF, poet and teacher at the University of California, published his first collection of verse shortly before the appearance of his essay on Miss Moore's prosody.

R. P. BLACKMUR, critic and poet, includes among his works *The Double Agent* and *Language as Gesture*.

KENNETH BURKE, critic and poet, is the author of *A Grammar of Motives*, perhaps his most famous single work.

DENIS DONOGHUE has published *The Third Voice*, a study of modern verse drama. His *Connoisseurs of Chaos* deals with American poetry from Whitman to the present; *The Ordinary Universe* is a sequel to that book. He is Professor of English at University College, Dublin.

T. S. ELIOT scarcely needs introduction. His two pieces on Miss Moore have been difficult to come by for many years. Marianne Moore's essay on Eliot appears in *Predilections*.

HENRY GIFFORD, author of *The Novel in Russia, Comparative Literature*, and a body of articles on Russian and chiefly modern literature, is Winterstoke Professor of English at the University of Bristol.

HUGH KENNER, author of many books on modern literature, has written important studies of Pound, Wyndham Lewis, Joyce, Eliot, and Beckett. He teaches at the University of California.

RANDALL JARRELL, poet, critic and novelist, has a variety of essays on modern poetry in his *Poetry and the Age* and has written a second essay on Miss Moore that is not reprinted in this volume.

RICHARD A. MACKSEY teaches at Johns Hopkins University in the Writing Seminars. He has published his own poetry and a number of critical articles on modern literature.

HOWARD NEMEROV, poet and critic, formulated the questions to which Miss Moore supplied the answers in a pamphlet not given here, *Poetry and Criticism* (see Selected Bibliography).

R. H. PEARCE, in addition to editing Whitman's *Leaves of Grass* (1860 text), has written a lengthy study of American poetry from Puritan times, *The Continuity of American Poetry*.

EZRA POUND "discovered" many of the major literary talents of this century including Eliot, Joyce, and Miss Moore. Marianne Moore has included an essay on Pound's *A Draft of XXX Cantos* in *Predilections.*

JOHN CROWE RANSOM, poet and critic, prominent in the revival of Southern literature, edited *The Kenyon Review* for many years.

WALLACE STEVENS also writes interestingly to and about Miss Moore in his *Letters.* See particularly the letter to T. C. Wilson of March 25, 1935.

WILLIAM CARLOS WILLIAMS gives interesting glimpses of Miss Moore both in his *Autobiography* and in *I Wanted to Write a Poem.*

Selected Bibliography

An essential document is Sheehy, Eugene P., and Kenneth A. Lohf, *The Achievement of Marianne Moore: A Bibliography 1907–1957* (New York: New York Public Library, 1958).

Bogan, Louise, *Achievement in American Poetry, 1900–1950* (Chicago: Henry Regnery Co., 1951), *passim.*

Cole, Thomas, "The Revised Poems of Marianne Moore," *Imagi,* VI, No. I (1952), 11–12.

Engle, Bernard F., *Marianne Moore* (New York: Twayne Publishers, Inc., 1964).

Garrigue, Jean, *Marianne Moore,* University of Minnesota Pamphlets on American Writers, No. 50 (Minneapolis: University of Minnesota Press, 1965).

Gregory, Horace, and Marya A. Zaturenska, "Marianne Moore: the Genius of *The Dial,*" *The History of American Poetry, 1900–1940* (New York: Harcourt, Brace & World, Inc., 1946), pp. 317–25.

Hoffman, Daniel G., "Moore's 'See in the midst of fair leaves,'" *Explicator,* X (March, 1952), 34.

Hoffman, Frederick J., *The Twenties: American Writing in the Postwar Decade* (New York: The Viking Press, Inc., 1955), pp. 176–79, 260–61, and *passim.*

Jarrell, Randall, "The Humble Animal," *Kenyon Review,* IV (Autumn, 1942) 408–11. Reprinted in *The Kenyon Critics: Studies in Modern Literature from the Kenyon Review,* ed. John Crowe Ransom (Cleveland: The World Publishing Company, 1951), pp. 277–80. Also reprinted in Jarrell's *Poetry and the Age* (New York: Alfred A. Knopf, Inc., 1953), pp. 179–84.

———, "Thoughts about Marianne Moore," *Partisan Review,* XIX (November–December, 1952), 687–700.

Leavis, F. R., "Marianne Moore," *Scrutiny,* IV, No. 1 (1935), 87–90.

"Marianne Moore Issue," *Quarterly Review of Literature,* IV, No. 2 (1948), 121–223. Guest editor: José Garcia Villa.

Monroe, Harriet, "Symposium on Marianne Moore," *Poetry,* XIX (January, 1922), 208–16.

Moore, Marianne, and Howard Nemerov, *Poetry and Criticism* (Cambridge, Mass.: Adams House and Lowell House, 1965).

Munson, Gorham Bert, "Marianne Moore," *Destinations; a Canvass of American Literature Since 1900* (New York: J. H. Sears, 1928), pp. 90–100.

Pound, Ezra. *Letters, 1907–1941,* ed. D. D. Paige (New York: Harcourt, Brace & World, Inc., 1950), *passim.*

Rosenfeld, Paul, "Marianne Moore," in *Men Seen; Twenty-four Modern Authors* (New York: Lincoln MacVeagh, Dial Press, 1925), pp. 165–73.

Schulman, Grace, "Conversation with Marianne Moore," *Quarterly Review of Literature,* XVI, Nos. 1–2 (1969), pp. 154–71.

Southworth, James Granville, "Marianne Moore," in *More Modern American Poets* (New York: The Macmillan Company, Oxford: William Blackwell & Sons Ltd., 1954), pp. 41–48.

Stevens, Wallace, "A Poet that Matters," in *Life and Letters Today,* XIII (December, 1935), 61–65. Reprinted in *Opus Posthumous* (New York: Alfred A. Knopf, Inc., 1957), pp. 247–54.

Taupin, René, "Marianne Moore," *L'Influence du Symbolisme Francais sur la Poesie Américaine* (Paris: H. Champion, 1929), pp. 273–75.

Tomlinson, Charles, "Abundance, not too much: the Poetry of Marianne Moore," *Sewanee Review,* LXV (Autumn, 1957), 677–87.

Winters, Yvor, "Holiday and Day of Wrath," *Poetry,* XXVI (April, 1925), 39–44.

———, *In Defense of Reason* (Denver: University of Denver Press, 1947), *passim.*

Zabel, Morton Dauwen, "A Literalist of the Imagination," *Poetry,* XLVII (March, 1936), 326–36. Reprinted in *Literary Opinion in America* (New York: Harper & Row, Publishers, 1951), pp. 385–92.

CHARLES TOMLINSON, the editor of this volume in the Twentieth Century Views series, is currently a Reader in English poetry at the University of Bristol, England. He has received numerous awards for his own poetry as well as having written many essays on other works of literature.

DEMCO, INC. 38-2931